Original title:
Dreams Beneath a Winter Sky

Author: Penelope Hawthorne
ISBN HARDBACK: 978-9916-94-578-0
ISBN PAPERBACK: 978-9916-94-579-7

Portraits of Stillness in Snow-Capped Time

Snowflakes dance like little clowns,
Twirling down to paint the towns.
Frosty faces in a winter play,
Tickling noses as they sway.

Beneath the Celestial Shroud

The stars wink at frosty toes,
As chilly bobbles on my nose.
Snowmen giggle, hats askew,
Wearing mittens just for hue.

The Winter's Wistful Canvas

Icicles hang like frozen cheer,
Whispering secrets to the deer.
The trees are dressed in white delight,
Where squirrels plan a snowball fight.

A Symphony of Snowy Silence

Beneath the hush of downy flakes,
The world prepares for silly wakes.
Balloons of snow atop my head,
It's time to laugh, not stay in bed!

Moonlit Chills and Unseen Hopes

A penguin slips in frosty air,
He twirls and twirls without a care.
A snowman giggles, hat askew,
As snowflakes giggle, falling too.

Starry nights with squirrels in flight,
Playing tag in shimmering light.
With snowballs flying, laughter loud,
Winter's whimsy makes us proud.

Frostbitten Fantasies in the Stillness

A polar bear in bright pink shades,
Dances while playing karaoke fades.
Chasing snowflakes like they're a treat,
Wearing ice skates on furry feet.

Bunnies hop wearing fluffy hats,
Cozy jokes traded with chitchats.
In the stillness, silliness sings,
As winter's magic merrily clings.

Twilight's Embrace in the Cold

The owl in a scarf gives a hoot,
While mice on skis zoom around in pursuit.
Chilly breezes, a tickle to the nose,
Ticklish snowflakes land on toes.

Hot cocoa laughs as marshmallows dive,
In a cup full of giggles, they thrive.
Twilight glows under a toasty cheer,
A winter wonderland floors with glee, dear.

The Aurora's Secret Embrace

A bear with dreams, a bright-spoken wish,
Chased by auroras, oh how they swish!
Snowmen breakdance, grooves in the night,
While frosty vines twirl out of sight.

Whispering winds tell tales that jest,
Of hearty laughter from east to west.
In colors bright under chilly clime,
Winter's mischief dances out of time.

Reflections on a Frozen Pond

A duck in a hat struts with style,
While fish beneath chuckle, going a mile.
They roll in circles, creating a scene,
Who knew ice could be such a dream machine?

With snowflakes dancing like little dancers,
A squirrel slides in with comical glances.
He slips on the ice, does a pirouette,
Turns out winter's a stage, don't you forget!

Starry Nightfall Over White Landscapes

In the moon’s glow, the snowflakes shimmer,
While penguins paintball and the stars start to glimmer.
A snowman uprises with a carrot for nose,
With dreams of warm beaches, oh how it glows!

The owls gossip softly, sharing their tales,
Of awkward dear deer with boots and green veils.
They tiptoe and stumble, causing a stir,
Under the soft blanket where they dabble and purr.

Fantasies Wrapped in Winter's Embrace

The coffee mugs chatter in happy delight,
While marshmallows ski down the mugs, what a sight!
A snow angel giggles, flapping her wings,
While hot cocoa sings all its wintery things.

With snowflakes that tickle when they collide,
The cat joins a snow pile, feeling quite pride.
With whiskers a-twitch and a puff of a tail,
As snowmen declare that they'll never regale!

The Gentle Cradle of Snow

A blanket of snow, so fluffy and bright,
Hides the mischief of rabbits at night.
They hop and they skip, with flurries of cheer,
While a fox in pajamas pretends he's a deer.

Frosty yawned, not quite ready to freeze,
While squirrels held parties, snacking on cheese.
They strut in the moonlight, proud as a king,
In a world full of giggles, oh what fun they bring!

Celestial Lullabies in a Frozen Realm

In a land where penguins sing,
Snowflakes dance and build a fling.
Chilly giggles fill the air,
As frostbite paints a funny glare.

Polar bears do pirouettes,
While frosty folks do silly bets.
Icicles hang like candy canes,
As snowmen tell their freezing tales.

The Serenity of Sleep under a Frigid Bliss.

Snuggled tight in cozy beds,
With warm socks upon our heads.
The winter winds blow loud and clear,
Tickling noses, bringing cheer.

Snoozing cats on window sills,
Chasing dreams of frosty thrills.
In a world of frozen jokes,
Where snowballs fling and laughter cloaks.

Silent Whispers of Frozen Nights

Snowflakes whisper with delight,
Telling tales of icy flight.
Squirrels wearing fuzzy hats,
Chuckle softly at the cats.

Under stars that shiver bright,
Frosty creatures join the night.
With snow angels making puns,
While the moonlight giggles funs.

Stardust on Snowflakes

Dancing lights on frosty eves,
As tiny fairies spin and weave.
Snowmen wearing silly crowns,
Twirling round in fluffy gowns.

Skiing squirrels, fast as can be,
Zooming 'round like they're on spree.
Each snowflake holds a goofy grin,
As winter's laughter doth begin.

Harmony in Temporary Thawing

Snowmen wobble with delight,
Their carrots start to droop right.
A snowball fight, oh what a mess,
Yet icy giggles still impress!

Winter sun, a fickle tease,
Chasing ice with gentle ease.
A puddle forms where snow once lay,
And slippery shoes lead us astray!

Hot cocoa spills, a fashion choice,
As marshmallows dance, rejoice!
Frosty noses, rosy cheeks,
Who knew winter could bring squeaks?

In this thaw, we laugh with glee,
Sledding down a hill, whee!
Joy in every slip and slide,
Can’t wait for spring to come outside!

Melodies of Nightfall and Snow

The snowflakes tango, quite a show,
While penguins wonder, 'Where to go?'
A serenade of chilly tunes,
As carolers sing to sleeping moons.

Frosty breath makes funny shapes,
As we waltz with snowman capes.
A sled flies past, what a sight,
'Don't eat the yellow snow!'—goodnight!

Noses red like ripe tomatoes,
Chasing after winter's shadows.
Caught in laughter, oh what fun,
As squirrels join the midnight run!

Snow boots squeak, a slippery dance,
In the frost, we take our chance.
With each giggle, spirits soar,
Winter's magic, what a lore!

Whirls of Fantasy on Frosty Grounds

A snowball flies, a voice does shout,
In frosted fields, there's never doubt.
Snowflakes spark like tiny lights,
In this winter, we take flights.

The dog's a blur, a snowy whiz,
Chasing fluff, in frosty fizz.
A snowshoe hare gives a wink,
While ice birds playfully clink!

Laughter echoes off the trees,
As we slip down snowy knees.
Frosted fingers try to catch,
The giggles that seem to hatch.

A winter tale, we spin and weave,
With sticks for swords, we dance, believe.
In this world of white delight,
We're kings and queens of frosty night!

The Painting of a Winter Reverie

With each flake, a stroke of art,
Nature's canvas, a playful heart.
Icicles hang like glittering pranks,
As frost paints the world in icy ganks.

A raccoon dons a cap of snow,
Hoping for a round of 'whoah!'
With mittens stuck in funny spots,
And leaping cats in chilly knots.

Slipping past a frozen fence,
While our laughter makes no sense.
In the woods, a bunny hops,
While chilly giggles never stop.

A carnival of chilly cheer,
Each moment bright, the sky so clear.
In this wonderland, we sway,
Wishing every snow would stay!

Chasing Silhouettes in the Snow

In a frosty freeze, we dart and dive,
Snowballs flying, we feel alive.
Sleds on hills, and giggles galore,
Who knew winter could be such a chore?

Snowmen wobble with carrot noses,
As we start to strike heroic poses.
Outfits bundled, looking quite round,
In this soft fluff, we lose and are found.

The night is cold but hearts are warm,
As we embark on our snowy swarm.
Faces aglow with laughter bright,
In this winter world, we take flight.

Frosted Horizons of Forgotten Wishes

With snowflakes dancing and swirling wide,
We make a splash, a fun-filled ride.
Wishes whispered to frosty trees,
As we bounce back from winter's freeze.

Our boots are chunky, we leap and twirl,
But who knew ice could send us in a whirl?
Tumbles galore, it's slapstick fun,
A frosted ballet has just begun.

Mittens mismatched, but spirits high,
Laughter echoes under the sky.
Whole worlds built from frosty delight,
In this silly show, we feel just right.

Whimsy Under the Blanket of Snow

Under white covers, we giggle and play,
Creating mischief in a gleeful display.
Snow angels flap with arms spread wide,
In this wonderland, we can’t hide.

Sledding down hills, a delightful scare,
Landing in snow, laughter fills the air.
Hot cocoa warms our cold little hands,
As we spin tales of magical lands.

Snowflakes tickle the end of our noses,
Painting the world with whimsical poses.
In this frosty maze of giggles and cheer,
Holiday silliness wraps us near.

The Luminous Veil of a Quiet Night

Under a blanket where snowflakes sleep,
Our giggles scatter, secrets we keep.
Silly shadows dance in the glow,
While winter stars twinkle below.

The moonlight laughs as snowflakes fall,
We tumble and roll, we give it our all.
With cheeks aglow, we prance all around,
In this quiet night, joy is profound.

Each step crunches in soft diamond light,
While whimsy takes wing, inviting delight.
We chase our laughter, oh what a thrill,
In this mesmerizing winter chill.

Hibernation of the Soul

Snuggled tight in blankets curled,
A bear's retreat in a cozy world.
The winter snacks around me piled,
A snack attack, I'm like a child.

Hot cocoa flows like joyful streams,
I sip and laugh at all my dreams.
In fuzzy socks, I prance and play,
While snowflakes dance, I'm here to stay.

The fridge is full, the couch my throne,
I rule this kingdom all alone.
With every snack, my laughter swells,
In hibernation, I cast my spells.

So come and join this lazy feat,
Let's turn our home into a treat.
With giggles echoing in the air,
We'll hibernate without a care.

Enchanted Slumbers under Crystal Canopies

Beneath the sheets, a fortress made,
In snow-white realms, my dreams parade.
I see a rabbit in a hat,
He hops away, imagine that!

Icicle castles in my mind,
Where silly penguins dance unlined.
They slip and slide, they twirl and glide,
With flippers flapping, oh what pride!

A polar bear with polka dots,
Breaks through my dreams, connects the dots.
He wears a scarf of plaid so bright,
A fashion guru in the night!

When morning comes and dreams take flight,
I'll laugh at tales from frozen night.
For in this land of winter fun,
Every day's a snowball run.

Shadows Dance on the Icy Canvas

The moonlight drips on frost-kissed ground,
Where shadows giggle without a sound.
They tiptoe lightly, side to side,
On frozen paths where secrets hide.

A snowman winks, his carrot grin,
I swear he just invited in…
A troupe of elves who peek and play,
They'll break the ice and seize the day!

With frosty doodles in the air,
Silly shapes beyond compare.
They twist and swirl, a merry band,
On nature's stage, all unplanned.

As morning glimmers, joy's revealed,
Those shadows laugh, their fate unsealed.
For every night, a tale to spin,
In winter's cloak, we all jump in!

Winter's Breath: A Tale of Loss and Wonder

The trees all dressed in winter's fluff,
They shrug and shake; it’s never enough.
But frostbite nibbles at my toes,
Oh, how the chilly wind just blows!

In search of warmth, I find a hat,
A fuzzy thing, it looks so fat.
With every step, it bounces round,
Like jelly beans on icy ground.

I chase the snowflakes, wild and bold,
But trip on sleigh bells made of gold.
Through laughter echoes, I confess,
Winter’s folly is a fun-filled mess!

Yet every slip, every small fall,
Creates a story — oh, what a ball!
So here’s to winter's frosty kiss,
In chilly moments, there’s pure bliss.

The Stillness of Shortened Days

The snowflakes dance, they spin and twirl,
While penguins waddle, giving a whirl.
Socks are slippers, what a grand sight,
There's magic in a mug, hot chocolate delight.

The frost on windows, a puzzling art,
Drawn by our breath, a creative heart.
Snowmen are laughing, their noses so bright,
Cursorily cheerful, with buttons in sight.

Fables Etched in White

Squirrels in jackets, they scamper and play,
Hiding their acorns, come what may.
A reindeer in a scarf, struts with such grace,
While elves are at work, in a snowball race.

The trees wear frosty hats, tall and grand,
A rabbit with shades has a sunbathing stand.
Even the clouds chuckle, puffed up and round,
As laughter in snowflakes softly resounds.

Flickers of Hope on Winter's Edge

Beneath the layers of frosty white,
Lurks a snail, unwilling to fight.
A snowball fight? A serious affair,
Though no one expects it, the cat will declare.

With mittens askew, we tumble and fall,
The snowman grins, he's seen it all.
And just when we tire, the sun peeks through,
Bringing giggles, and warmth anew.

Pathways to the Silent Dreamscape

Waffles by fire, a breakfast supreme,
While kids plan a heist for sugary cream.
Snow paths lead whispers through trees that twist,
While fairies giggle, you can’t quite resist.

Slippers slide on icy stages of fun,
Juggling hot cocoa, under the sun.
With each playful step in this wintery bliss,
We twirl and we laugh, not a moment to miss.

Chilling Delights of the Winter Night

Snowflakes dance on frosty ground,
Hot cocoa spills, oh what a sound!
Penguins tackle ice with flair,
Socks on noses, laughter's in the air.

Sleds crash loud, a snowy might,
Snowmen wobble, ready to fight!
Gloves in pockets, mittens lost,
Winter silliness at any cost.

Biting winds, but spirits high,
Snowball fights that make us fly!
The howling wind, a playful tease,
Life's a game, just feel the freeze.

Jack Frost's pranks, a cheeky glint,
Elves with mischief, oh how they glint!
In shivery fun, we'll stay awhile,
With snowmen grinning, we join the style.

The Illusion of Melting Stars

Stars above in frosty gleam,
Are they melting? What a dream!
Snowflakes mimic starry glow,
While hot tea spills in sleepy flow.

Cups of cheer, like ice we cheer,
With marshmallows floating near.
Scarf wrapped tight, we twirl about,
With giggles loud, we scream and shout.

Frosty faces, rosy red,
Laughter bubbling like warm bread.
Icicles drip, a chime of fun,
As winter games have just begun.

Trust the stars, they won't go far,
Out in the cold, we'll raise the bar!
For silly times beneath the light,
Even in frost, hearts feel just right.

Enigmas of a Frozen Horizon

Frosty puzzles, snowflakes fall,
Sled or surf? We can’t recall!
Chasing shadows, what a chase,
Snowball fights that make us race.

Hidden treasures in the snow,
Found a mitten? Let it flow!
Winter's cloak, so full of cheer,
It's magic time, come gather near.

Warming up with hot pie treats,
While penguins join us for our feats.
The frozen world holds quite a jest,
In silly games, we find our zest.

All in fun, we’ll never freeze,
With laughter ringing through the trees.
So leap and bounce, and let it fly,
In winter’s playground, we’ll reach the sky.

Glimmers in the Winter Haze

In the mist, a snowball flies,
A glimmer in a child’s eyes.
Snowman with a carrot nose,
Winks at us, as winter glows.

Whispers “whoopee” through the snow,
With snowshoes on, we steal the show!
Laughter echoes, icy fun,
As we chase the winter sun.

Frosty breaths and chilly eyes,
Try to catch the falling skies.
With laughter warm, like fireside,
In winter’s heart, we'll take a ride.

Winter haze, a magical game,
Snowflakes glisten, none the same.
In this chill, our hearts ignite,
With goofy grins, we shine so bright.

Frostbitten Journeys

With mittens mismatched, I step outside,
A penguin in my way, I must abide.
Snowballs fly like cats up in a tree,
Why does winter laugh at me, oh, why me?

Sleds are tangled like spaghetti strands,
I steer but end up in snowbank lands.
The snowman grins like he knows my plight,
As I tumble down, what a comical sight!

Hot cocoa spills on my woolen vest,
Spicy marshmallows put my skills to test.
Chasing after my hat, it flies away,
That gusty breeze sure loves to play!

I trade my boots for slippers in despair,
While snowflakes dance like they just don't care.
Winter's jokes are never quite so nice,
As I slip and slide on this frosty ice!

Enchanted Slumber Under Ice

The frost greets me with a giggle and grin,
While snowflakes twirl like they're trying to win.
In pajamas, I slip, slide, and glide,
Waking up to snow, oh, where do I hide?

Icicles dangle like candy canes,
I taste one and find it's got no gains.
The squirrels are plotting their winter heist,
As I bumble around, oh, what a feast!

I tripped on a snowball, my foot did a dance,
While winter whispered, “Just give it a chance.”
With a frosty breath and a chilly cheer,
What's hidden beneath this sky so eerily clear?

A snowman winks and steals my last bite,
Of pie left out for him on that fateful night.
I laugh to myself as I sip on my tea,
What a funny little world, just for me!

Celestial Gaze on Crystal Fields

Stars twinkling in the depths of the cold,
While I wear layers like an onion, so bold.
My toes are frozen, my fingers too,
Yet here I stand, what else can I do?

Sledding down hills with a laugh and a scream,
In a crash with a snowman — oh, what a dream!
He tumbles apart, and I'm left to grin,
"Sorry, my friend, let's drink beer and begin!"

With mittens on my ears, I shout to the moon,
"Can penguins sled? Are raccoons immune?"
The cosmos giggles, "What a fine query,
For those that slip, it's known quite clearly!"

As I dangle from branches, swinging with flair,
The snow captures laughter, like it's caught in the air.
In winter's embrace, with a wink and a cheer,
I dive into fun, for each moment is dear!

Snowy Veils of Midnight Thought

Under the stars in a blanket of white,
I ponder my choices while snuggled up tight.
To snowshoe or not, to scurry or breeze,
Muffins or cookies — oh, just bring me cheese!

The moonlight giggles as it pours like a drink,
While I find a snowdrift and come unlinked.
I tumble down softly, giggles abound,
Who knew wintry bliss brought such laughter around?

Gathering snowflakes that tickle my nose,
In search of the warmth that a hot pizza shows.
It's a culinary quest across blustery hills,
As I slip, trip, and laugh, oh, winter fulfills!

With frosty emblems and friends by my side,
Every minute a treasure, come take me for a ride.
So here's to the whimsy, the jests of the night,
In snowy veils of fun, everything feels just right!

Slumbering Visions in the Frost

In a world where snowflakes dance,
They twirl and giggle in their prance.
A snowman wears a silly hat,
He whispers jokes to the chatting cat.

The moon is sipping hot cocoa slow,
While penguins waddle to and fro.
A frosty tree is dressed in cheer,
With icicles that chime, loud and clear.

Squirrels in scarves serve ice cream cones,
While polar bears play on their phones.
A snowball fight begins with zest,
Even the frostbite joins the quest.

So wrap your dreams in blankets tight,
And laugh away the chilly night.
For in the frosty world's delight,
Laughter sparkles, oh what a sight!

A Canvas of Ice and Light

A painter spills his colors bright,
On gleaming surfaces of white.
Penguins sliding down the hill,
With feathered friends, they get their fill.

The trees are laughing, can you tell?
They're wearing snow like a fancy shell.
A playful fox with a bright red nose,
Is moonwalking while the winter glows.

Hot chocolate flows like rivers wide,
As marshmallows take the icy ride.
A snowflake lands on a puppy's head,
Who barks and pounces, then goes to bed.

The canvas glistens, oh what fun,
As snowmen twirl beneath the sun.
They throw a dance party every night,
In that chilly, sparkling light!

Nightfall's Lullaby in White

The stars are snoring, can you hear?
While frosty gnomes toss back a beer.
A pillow fight with snowflakes flung,
While lullabies are softly sung.

A bear wears PJs, snug and warm,
While rabbits giggle, causing alarm.
They toast to winter with cups held high,
As snowflakes chuckle and waltz by.

The night sky winks, a cheeky sight,
As shadows dance with sheer delight.
With every flake, a story’s spun,
In this soft hush, the fun’s begun.

So snuggle close, the tales unfold,
Amid the laughter, brave and bold.
For in the crisp, enchanted night,
The playful whispers take to flight!

The Stars are Shy Beneath the Clouds

The stars are peeking, full of grace,
Though clouds tickle them, just in case.
A roly-poly snowman sighs,
And makes up jokes that never dies.

Snowflakes dive like paratroopers,
As rabbits hop in feathered troopers.
They slip and slide with joyful squeaks,
Creating mischief every week.

As ice skaters spin, 'oh my!' they shout,
With hot cider warming, all about.
The moon’s a joker, casting light,
In this frosty world, laughter takes flight.

So gather 'round, both young and old,
In winter’s story, bright and bold.
For under this whimsical sky,
The stars get shy, but we all fly!

Chasing Shadows in Frosty Light

In a world where snowmen stand tall,
A penguin slips, takes a fall.
Snowflakes dance like silly sprites,
While mittens wage epic snowball fights.

Icicles hang like frozen spears,
Snowball missiles launched in cheers.
Chasing shadows, twirling with glee,
Wishing for more snow, oh let it be!

Frosty whiskers on my nose,
Waddle like a duck, who knows?
With laughter echoing through the air,
Winter's humor is beyond compare!

A snowman's carrot nose falls askew,
Uh oh, that wasn't the plan, who knew?
But with giggles and glistening eyes,
We'll gather 'round and share our tries.

Echoes of a Frost Kissed Reverie

A frosty morning, coffee in hand,
Mittens lost, I can hardly stand.
Pancakes fly like fluffy dreams,
As syrup spills in funny streams.

Snowflakes land on a dog’s nose,
He spins around, and winter goes!
Chasing after a bouncing ball,
Eating snow like it’s a free-for-all.

The old man waits to slip on ice,
But watch him groan, oh so precise!
Frosty windows with a grin,
All experiences pushed deep within.

With laughter ringing all around,
Noses rosy from playful sound.
We’ll make memories, oh what a spree,
In a frosty world, wild and free!

Lullabies of the Snowbound Moon

Under the moon, a snowball lands,
Right on top of unsuspecting hands.
Hot cocoa spills with a silly splat,
As we giggle, imagining that!

Beneath the twinkling, starry glow,
Pajamas clad for a show of snow.
A snow angel flaps, takes off in flight,
While rabbits hop with sheer delight.

Granny cackles with glee, oh dear,
As she builds a fort to hide her cheer.
Laughter bounces off the frozen trees,
With whispers of joy carried on the breeze.

As winter nights wear fluffy gowns,
We dance through icicles and frozen towns.
Each giggle sweet, like a lullaby tune,
Beneath the playful, snowbound moon.

Hibernation of Hope

In a cozy nook, all tucked away,
Snuggled up for a winter play.
The cat purrs loud, a king on his throne,
While I dream of snowflakes, soft as foam.

We joke that bears have it all wrong,
Hibernating through winter feels too long!
Peeking out for snacks, make no mistake,
The only hibernation I want is cake!

Snowdrifts piled up, like a pillow stack,
While squirrels plot for a squirrel attack.
Telling tales, we nibble and munch,
As we embrace the winter crunch!

Through chuckles, we find warmth anew,
In every yarn spun with a view.
With love and laughter, we'll always cope,
In this frosty season, a hibernation of hope!

Frosted Horizons of Unseen Desires

Snowmen wear hats that flop,
Sleds that tumble and skip, drop.
Cold air tickles, noses turn red,
While penguins in coats dance ahead.

Icicles hang like toothy grins,
Snowball fights lead to playful sins.
Hot cocoa spills, marshmallows dive,
Laughing together, oh, how we thrive!

Frosty breath in a puffing cloud,
Over the chaos, we feel so proud.
Unseen wishes in the frost, they play,
With each falling flake, joy leads the way.

Polar bears laugh, they cannot resist,
While snowflakes swirl, we all coexist.
In this winter, oh, what a spree,
Horizons frosted, full of glee!

Secrets in the Snowdrifts

Snowdrifts whisper tales so sly,
Of penguin prances and snowflakes that fly.
Frosty footprints lead us away,
To secret parties where snowmen sway.

Under the stars, a snowball duel,
As snowflakes laugh, the night's a fool.
Jackets zipped up, scarves tightly knotted,
Hidden snacks in pockets, oh, who plotted?

Frosty secrets wrapped in the night,
Where snowflakes giggle and take flight.
Snow angels giggle, tipped by a grin,
As cocoa spills, let the fun begin!

The moonlight glimmers on ice so bright,
As we flail and slip in slippery delight.
With every flake that tickles our toes,
In snowdrifts, oh, joy endlessly grows!

Laced with Silver in the Chill

Laughter dances in the icy air,
With snowflakes laced in winter flair.
Frosted fingers, mittens in play,
As snowmen plot their sneaky sway.

Sliding down hills, we scream with glee,
While squirrels throw acorns, oh dear me!
Gloves all soggy, boots filled with snow,
Yet we prance around with delightful glow.

Beneath the chill, fun's always near,
With cocoa cheers that fill us with cheer.
Each snowflake spins a twisty tale,
As we revel, our worries pale.

Winter's canvas, painted so bright,
Whimsical whispers, pure delight.
In silver laces, we find our thrill,
Chasing laughter in the frosty still.

Cocoa Wishes and Winter Kisses

Hot cocoa winks from a steaming mug,
As winter tricks us, giving a hug.
Marshmallows bob like silly heads,
While snowflakes tickle like playful threads.

Fires crackle and giggles erupt,
As snowflakes dance like kittens, corrupt.
A sledding race, who will win?
With winter kisses, let the fun begin!

Cookie crumbs trail from the kitchen,
Frosted laughter is often glitchin'.
Socks mismatched and faces aglow,
In this chilly chaos, we steal the show.

Fueled by wishes, sugary spice,
Winter's blanket feels so nice.
Through laughter and cocoa, our hearts ignite,
As we savor the secrets of this snowy night.

Whispers of the Northern Wind

Snowflakes dance in silly glee,
They tiptoe 'round the old oak tree.
A snowman winks, a carrot nose,
He tells a joke that nobody knows.

Sledding down the hill, such fun,
A tumble here, oh, what a run!
Hot cocoa spills, marshmallows fly,
We laugh until we nearly cry.

Icicles dangle, dripping fate,
Is that a penguin? No, it’s a mate!
With mittens mismatched, we play tag,
As laughter rolls, our spirits wag.

So here’s to winter, bright and bold,
With tales of wonder yet untold.
Let’s twirl and swirl in frosty air,
And find the joy that's everywhere.

Frost-Touched Reveries

In a world of ice, where penguins dance,
I slipped on snow, lost my chance!
An owl hoots, “Get up, my friend!”
But I’m too busy on this trend.

Snowballs fly in a playful fight,
Two dogs chase after with pure delight.
The cat looks on, all fierce and grand,
Plotting to join, but not as planned.

A frosty branch caught in a pie,
I wonder, did it just fly by?
Each frosty breath is a puff of cheer,
While hot pies warm my winter sphere.

Beneath a sky of sparkling sheen,
We laugh out loud with frosty scene.
So grab your hats, hold onto tight,
For winter’s whims are pure delight!

A Tapestry of Icy Dreams

A field of snow, a canvas wide,
Where snowmen flex, and sledges glide.
Frosty whispers fill the air,
While snowflakes twirl without a care.

Winter's magic, a silly prank,
A squirrel's chattering, what a crank!
Laughter echoes through the trees,
As children tumble with such ease.

Giggling foxes in a chase,
A polar bear in a tutu grace.
Igloos sprout in vibrant hues,
As snowball fights create the news.

So dance with frost, let your heart sing,
For winter fun is a wondrous thing.
In this icy realm, we find our way,
To joy and laughter, come what may.

Frosted Notes on the Wind

A chilly tune floats through the air,
With frosty giggles, we all share.
A snowflake lands upon my nose,
I sneeze, and chaos quickly grows.

The penguins slide on icy slope,
While smiling squirrels weave their hope.
A mischief-maker in the tree,
Throws acorns down; it's pure folly!

Snowshoes clomp like giant frogs,
As laughter rolls, the cold it jogs.
Woolly hats with pompoms bright,
Having fun, from day to night.

In this frosty world, we find delight,
With each frolic, oh what a sight!
Let's sing and laugh as snowflakes fall,
For winter's magic enchants us all.

Celestial Frost and Quiet Wishes

In the chill, we laugh and sway,
Snowflakes dance in a comical way.
Sweaters clash like colors bright,
Snowmen wobble, what a sight!

Mittens lost in a snowy creek,
Frozen noses, we can't speak.
Twinkling stars above our heads,
Counting snowballs instead of beds.

Sleds go tumbling down the lane,
Laughter echoing, what a gain!
Frosty eyebrows, giggles burst,
Hot cocoa next, oh what a thirst!

Chasing snowflakes, we don't care,
Making angel shapes in the air.
Winter fun, we can't deny,
In this frost, we learn to fly!

Hushed Voices in the Snow

Whispers float on the frosty breeze,
A snowball fight brings us to our knees.
Slipping, sliding, laughter loud,
Even penguins would be proud!

Footprints lead where the snowflakes fall,
A secret path, we heed the call.
Hot pies waiting at the end,
The perfect treat from a winter friend!

Snowflakes kiss our noses cold,
As we huddle, not feeling bold.
The chilly air makes us sing,
Oh, the joy that winter brings!

With every giggle, the snowflakes twirl,
Round and round in a frosty whirl.
Kites of ice against the night,
What a way to end our flight!

Whispers from the Frosted Pines

Frosty whispers through the trees,
Chattering squirrels aim to please.
Snow-covered branches bend and sway,
Watch out below, we might play!

Hot potatoes in woolly socks,
Making bets on frozen blocks.
Yetis dance, or so they say,
Join the fun, don’t stray away!

A snow angel flops on the ground,
While giggling friends gather 'round.
Frosty eyebrows raise in surprise,
Caught mid-snowball, what a prize!

As the night covers the land,
Mirth and laughter go hand in hand.
Under starlit skies, we find,
A frosty wonderland, so kind!

Celestial Dreams in the Cold Embrace

A frosty moon with a cheeky grin,
Shimmers down on all our spins.
Snowflakes twirl like silly sprites,
Dancing under chilly lights!

Sleds turn sideways, laughter spills,
Rolling kids on snowy hills.
Round the fire with warm delights,
Sharing stories of winter nights.

Snowmen sport our hats and ties,
Looks like they planned a grand surprise!
Two noses stuck, and one fell down,
We're the best frosty circus in town!

With cocoa served in cups so wide,
Who could keep these giggles inside?
In the cold where laughter plays,
We’ll stay in this joy-filled haze!

A Shiver of Stars Above

Snowflakes dance like silly sprites,
They slip and slide on frosty nights.
With every twirl, they laugh and spin,
Creating messes, oh what a win!

A snowman's scarf, a goofy sight,
With mismatched buttons, oh what delight.
His carrot nose, a crooked grin,
In this white world, let antics begin!

Distant stars twinkle with cheeky glee,
As snowflakes play tag, just wait and see.
Under the moon, the fun won't cease,
Through frosty mischief, we find our peace.

So come and join this playful scene,
Where laughter reigns and joy's routine.
Beneath the shiver, let's find our song,
In this winter wonder, we all belong.

Impressions of Winter’s Heart

The chill arrives with a puff and blow,
Sending hats flying, what a show!
A mittens’ chase down the icy lane,
Laughter erupts as they slide again.

An oversized coat, two sizes too wide,
It wiggles and jiggles with every stride.
Socks on hands, what a silly fear,
Fashion statements in the frosty sphere!

Snowball fights launch with comical flair,
Each throw a mission to drench with care.
With cheeks ablaze, there’s no retreat,
In the battle of snow, no one’s discreet!

So sip some cocoa, let’s warm our hearts,
In this winter game, the fun never departs.
With snowflakes twirling, and joyful art,
The season’s laughter is winter’s sweet part.

Frosty Echoes of Forgotten Realms

Icicles dangle like frozen charms,
Beware the drip; it has its harms!
A holiday hat caught on a branch,
What a riot with every chance!

Sledding down hills brings shouts of glee,
As we race past trees, just you and me.
With every bump and bound we take,
Our giggles echo, for fun’s own sake.

Pine trees wear hats made of snow,
Comical figures that put on a show.
Nature’s laughter lights up the scene,
As frosty echoes keep spirits keen.

So let’s bundle up, and venture forth,
Through this chilly realm of playful mirth.
With frozen memories and smiles so bright,
In every heartbeat, we chase the light.

Lanterns Lit by Northern Lights

The sky’s ablaze with colors bold,
Like paint spilled high, oh what a hold!
With lanterns swaying, they greet the night,
In this canvas of stars, everything's bright.

Snowmen wobble, with arms askew,
Each one a character, just like you.
With drunken stumbles, they bring us cheer,
In this winter tale, there’s nothing to fear!

Penguins in boots slide on the ice,
Their waddle and giggles sure entice.
We join their silliness, hearts all aglow,
In a world where laughter continues to flow.

So gather ‘round, let laughter ring,
With frosty giggles and the joy they bring.
In the northern glow, let’s dance tonight,
For who knew winter could be this bright?

Whispers of Snowflakes at Dusk

Snowflakes dance in swirling glee,
A chilly waltz for you and me.
They tickle noses, laugh with cheer,
As we glide past, with frozen beer.

The snowman grins with carrot nose,
While whispered secrets he overthrows.
With hats too big, and scarves askew,
He quips, 'I’m warmer than all of you!'

Cocoa spills from mugs in hand,
A chocolate avalanche, oh so grand.
As marshmallows float like fluffy ships,
We giggle with hot drinks on our lips.

Beneath the twilight’s frosty cloak,
We share our warmth, and tell a joke.
So come, dear friend, let’s roam outside,
With snowflakes swirling, our hearts collide.

Frosted Reflections of the Heart

The mirror of ice reflects our glee,
With frosty faces like a winter spree.
We catch our breath in frozen air,
And wish for mittens we forgot to wear.

Icicles cheer from rooftops high,
"Don't slip too much, or you'll say goodbye!"
While sleds race down the snowy hills,
Our laughter echoes, oh what thrills!

With cheeks aglow from winter fun,
We shout, "More snow! This day's just begun!"
Snowball fights bring laughter loud,
As we dodge, duck, and spin, so proud.

The frosted window paints a scene,
Of holidays past, of frosty sheen.
With hugs and smiles amid the chill,
We find warm joy, the heart to fill.

The Silent Vigil of the Stars

The stars twinkle like giggling lights,
Atop a world that seems just right.
The moon peeks down with a wink and grin,
As if to say, 'Come on, let's begin!'

Snowflakes catch the cosmic glow,
And sprinkle down from skies so low.
Each flake a joke in a frosty dance,
Making even grumps take a chance.

In the stillness, we shiver and sway,
Under the blanket of twinkly play.
While crickets chirp, an icy sound,
Their winter tune, delight profound.

We open our hearts to the night so clear,
Sharing our hopes, and winter cheer.
With laughter bright, and skies so vast,
We savor moments that always last.

Echoes of a Chilling Reverie

Whispers of ice create a tune,
As frostbite sneezes 'achoo!' by noon.
The snowflakes giggle as they descend,
'Catch us if you can, dear friend!'

Each breath exhales in puffs of white,
As we stumble on in jolly flight.
With scarves flying high like flags at war,
We race through drifts, hearts wanting more.

The trees wear hats of crystal white,
While squirrels chuckle at our plight.
In the frosty air, our laughter rings,
While the winter air tickles like giggling springs!

As night drifts in with stars aglow,
We gather close, the warmth in tow.
So here's to winters that sparkle and freeze,
With echoes of fun carried on the breeze.

Aurora of Silent Wishes

Snowflakes dance like silly sprites,
While hot cocoa steals our sights.
The snowman grins with a carrot nose,
Hoping that frostbite won't impose.

Underneath the twinkling stars,
A penguin dreams of shiny cars.
Snowball fights turn into flops,
As snowmen play hopscotch with pops.

Chasing shadows in the night,
Wrapped in scarves, we feel so bright.
The chill can’t freeze the laughter here,
As we mock the frost with winter cheer.

In this frozen wonderland,
Sledding takes a silly stand.
With each faceplant, giggles soar,
Who knew snow could be such a bore?

Frosted Breath of Serenity

Puffing clouds from my lips I see,
Is that a walrus winking at me?
As icicles dangle like frozen tears,
I chuckle while battling my fears.

Hot chocolate spills on the ground,
As I slip on ice without a sound.
Snow angels flutter, arms in flight,
While deer in the distance share a fright.

Inflatable igloos make us laugh,
As penguins cavort just like a giraffe.
Snickers echo through frosty air,
While ducks in jackets strut with flair.

Under the sky's frosty dismay,
We stumble about in a classy way.
With hearts so light, we embrace the cold,
And frosted fun turns funny and bold.

Lanterns of Light in the Wintry Dark

The lanterns sway in winter's breeze,
As squirrels hold winter tea parties with ease.
Snowflakes giggle as they land,
On fuzzy hats and snowball stands.

While raccoons gather under moonlight's kiss,
They're crafting snow cones, you can't miss.
A frosty rabbit hops ‘round in glee,
Donning a scarf that's far too free.

The stars are blushing like brides in white,
While we chase shadows, oh what a sight!
With snowball dodges and flurry of spins,
Winter fun is where the laughter begins.

So light a fire, let's roast some s'mores,
Maybe the raccoons will knock at our doors.
Under twinkling skies, let joy take flight,
In this frosty land of pure delight.

Murmurs of the Cold Twilight

Whispers dance on frosty air,
With penguins waltzing everywhere.
The moon snickers, a cheeky sprite,
As the snowflakes gather for a snowball fight.

Icicles hang with a sassy flair,
While winter critters plot in their lair.
The chill brings joy, a silly muse,
As we form snowmen with mismatched shoes.

Underneath a blanket of bright white,
We ponder snow's strange appetite.
Could snowmen rise for a midnight snack?
Or would they crumble and fade to black?

So we tiptoe through the soft, sparkly fluff,
With giggles that echo, isn't this tough?
In the twilight, laughter takes its toll,
As we collect memories, forever whole.

Moonlight's Dance on a Frosty Lake

Under the moon, the ice does sway,
A penguin in skates starts to play.
Chasing a fish, he slips with a grin,
A wild waltz begins as he falls with a spin.

Snowflakes giggle, they swirl in the air,
As snowmen dance without any care.
A carrot-nosed chap prances about,
With snowy amigos, he spins all about.

Frogs in tuxedos croak songs of delight,
While stars start to twinkle, oh what a sight!
The lake is a stage, each critter a star,
Under this frost, they shine near and far.

When morning arrives, they all take a seat,
At a table of snowballs, that's quite a treat.
With laughter and antics, they share all their tales,
Of frosty escapades and snowy gales.

Shadows of Whimsy on the Snow

In shadows that dance, a rabbit hops high,
Wearing a hat that's too big for a guy.
With boots made of marshmallows, he prances with flair,
Leaving funny paw prints for others to share.

A snowman with sunglasses catches a breeze,
He's chilling in style, doing as he please.
With a sombrero that floats on his round head,
He juggles some snowballs instead of bread.

A bear rolls a snowball that's much too immense,
He tumbles and chuckles—what a fun suspense!
Birds chirp in laughter as wintertime plays,
They swing in the trees with acorn bouquets.

The shadows grow long as night takes its claim,
And laughter echoes like a whimsical game.
In the blanket of white, each spirit aligns,
With joy in their hearts, beneath icy designs.

Fabled Dreams in the Winter's Hand

With snowflakes like whispers, he tiptoes about,
A dog in a scarf, filled with joy and no doubt.
He chases those flakes as they fall from the sky,
In a whirlwind of laughter, he jumps up high.

A cat on a sled, oh what a sight,
With goggles so big, she's ready for flight.
She glides down the slope with a giggle and cheer,
As mice in the snow cheer her on from near.

A moose with a mustache struts with great pride,
He's a king of the frosty, snowy glide.
With sleigh bells for shoes, his dance is a riot,
Each twirl and each leap, oh, he's quite the diet!

As night falls again, and the stars start to peek,
The critters take turns, each daring to speak.
In tales shared around, every chuckle a gift,
Winter's whimsy can cause quite the uplift.

Beneath the Icy Canopy

Under the branches of frost-laden trees,
A squirrel with style spins in the breeze.
With acorns for hats and twirls galore,
He tickles a pine cone—what fun he explores!

Nearby on a branch, a fox in a bow,
Tells tales to the owls about winter's glow.
With a wink and a nod, the night's filled with laughs,
As shadows join in for playful, warm drafts.

A turtle in mittens crawls slow but sure,
With snowflakes for confetti, his heart feels pure.
He slides on his shell, oh what a delight,
While bunnies applaud in the flickering light.

As the moon chuckles softly, the world spins with glee,
Under frosty blankets, the joy sets them free.
In winter's embrace, the magic unfolds,
With whimsy and laughter, each moment he holds.

Paths of Quietude in Winter's Grasp

Beneath the blankets of fluffy white,
Squirrels plot mischief, it’s quite a sight.
They march in a row, with small, nutty treats,
While I trip on ice, it's all but defeat.

Snowmen look dapper, all dressed up nice,
Yet, one took a tumble and slipped on some ice.
I laughed so hard, I fell right back down,
Who knew winter could make me a clown?

Penguins in mittens start a snowball fight,
While robins gossip, it’s quite a delight.
The snowflakes giggle as they twirl and glide,
While I chase my hat that has blown off with pride.

So here in the cold with a grin ear to ear,
I find joy in laughter, my heart full of cheer.
For winter's a canvas where giggles unfold,
In each chilly moment, it's warmth that I hold.

The Stillness Between Snowflakes

In the hush of the evening, snowflakes parade,
They flit through the air like kids unafraid.
I sip on hot cocoa, it spills on my shoe,
Perhaps my warm sweater needs some warming too!

Icicles hang like whiskers, quite funny to see,
I swear some are laughing directly at me.
Snowballs are weapons in battles we wage,
But tripping on ice is still all the rage.

With every soft flap of the cardinal's wing,
I chuckle aloud, what joy they can bring!
The world's a cold circus, with laughter so bright,
In the stillness of snow, joy takes gentle flight.

So let’s frolic and tumble without a care,
Life's a snow globe, full of magic to share.
While winter may chill, it warms up the soul,
With smiles and giggles, we dance to its roll.

Reflections of a Wintry Soul

The mirror of frost, with a grin, it does show,
A penguin in a bowtie, sliding down slow.
While I in my boots, flail about on the ground,
In a winter ballet that looks quite unsound.

Snowflakes joke and wink, like they're up to some fun,
Daring me to join them, oh, I can't be outdone!
But alas, as I tiptoe, I end up asked to waltz,
With a cushion of snow, it’s one massive default!

Hot chocolate erupts in a silly old mess,
I squirrel away treats that I must confess.
While snowmen chuckle, their noses askew,
It’s the laughter that binds us in winter’s cold dew.

So come one and all, let the giggles cascade,
For winter's a joke that just shan't ever fade.
In the chill of the night, we shall brighten the air,
With memories of laughter, and warmth that we share.

Fireflies of Memory in the Cold

Winter's a blanket of stories untold,
With laughter that dances and never grows old.
The fireflies of memory flicker and glow,
As I fumble and fidget in half-hearted show.

I shoved on my mittens, but one won't behave,
It slips from my finger like it's trying to save.
While the snowflakes twirl and whirl around me,
I chuckle at mischief that's clearly so free.

A snowball attempt goes awry, what a throw!
It splats on my neighbor, and oh, what a show!
With laughter echoing, loud muffled by snow,
I shake off the cold as I tumble below.

So here's to the moments of giggles and cheer,
To the fun in the frost when our hearts are sincere.
Though winter might chill, we find warmth in our glee,
In the fireflies of memory, we twirl with surre.

Starlit Sojourns in the Cold

Under twinkling stars, we roam,
In jackets puffy as a cloud.
Chasing snowflakes like a gnome,
Laughing loudly, feeling proud.

Icicles dangle like sharp teeth,
A penguin waddle on the go.
With every slide, we lose our breath,
Who knew ice made us so slow?

Snowmen grinning, eyes of coal,
They wink beneath the moonlit haze.
But watch your step, they might just roll,
And start a snowball-throwing craze!

So let's toast marshmallows bright,
Sipping cocoa, cheers in sight.
For winter nights are quite the sight,
When fun and laughter take their flight.

Veils of White and Whispers Untold

A flurry dances, oh such grace,
As snowflakes tease with icy jests.
We stumble, slip, fall on our face,
But laughter warms us like a nest.

Snow angels sprawled in pure delight,
Spreading wings in winter's bed.
Each flake dashes, a silly flight,
While snowmen plot their mischief ahead!

Hot cocoa flows in paper cups,
Marshmallows float like little boats.
We toast to winter's small hiccups,
As snowballs fly and laughter gloats.

So gather round, good friends, be bold,
As veils of white make stories told.
In every snowman's smile, behold,
The joy this chilly world can hold.

The Ethereal Comfort of Frosty Nights

In blankets thick and cocoa dreams,
The frosty air gives cheeks a glow.
With snowflakes tumbling in mad schemes,
We shout and cheer, our hearts aglow.

Neighbors’ lights twinkle like fireflies,
While winter whispers cheeky cheer.
We dance in coats, let out loud sighs,
As penguins train, we play with fear.

Laughter echoes like an old song,
As we build forts, victorious pride.
But in the snow, our footing’s wrong,
And down we go, our grace denied!

Yet frost gives warmth, a quirky line,
In every slip, in every bump.
So gather close, our jokes divine,
Laughing ’til we all feel thump.

Encounters with Ghosts of Winter's Past

A frosty breeze tells tales long lost,
Of winters filled with snowball fights.
Ghosts of snowmen, with arms embossed,
Chase us through these chilly nights.

They beckon with their carrot noses,
A flicker of mischief in their eyes.
We throw some snow, the spirit dozes,
And laughter shatters the quiet skies.

Hot cider's sipped, with cinnamon swirls,
As stories spill like melted snow.
Winter friends, in giddy whirls,
Chasing memories, to and fro.

So let's embrace these spectral pranks,
For winter's ghosts, they know us well.
In jokes and jests, let's give our thanks,
For every frosty tale they tell.

Memories Hushed in Crystal Stillness

Puffs of smoke and frosty air,
A penguin snores without a care.
Snowflakes fall like tiny pies,
Tickling noses, oh what a surprise!

Sleds go flying, giggles loud,
While snowmen dance, so very proud.
Hot cocoa spills, a chocolate lake,
Who knew winter could cause such a shake?

Icicles dangle, sharp as a knife,
But they can't cut through all this life.
Laughter bursts like bubbles in snow,
Winter's funny, don't you know?

So grab your hat and fuzzy gloves,
Let’s frolic where the cold wind shoves.
In this frosty, flurried round,
Laughter echoes all around.

Frost and the Dance of Wanted Dreams

Snowflakes tap dance on frozen pies,
While squirrels plot in furry disguise.
The rabbit hops in a woolly hat,
Chasing his tail, oh imagine that!

Frosted windows frame the show,
While penguins waddle, moving slow.
Thick mittens cover silly hands,
What madcap fun in snowy lands!

Cold noses kiss the chilly air,
As laughter rings, a joyful flare.
The snowman jigs, a sight to see,
Wobbling like he’s had too much tea!

So join the dance, don’t be shy,
Under the sparkle of winter's sky.
With giggles bright and hearts aglow,
Let the frost and fun freely flow!

Halos of Light Beneath White Canopies

Beneath the glow of lantern bright,
Icicles shimmer in crisp moonlight.
The trees wear crowns of glistening snow,
As laughter erupts in a frosty show.

A snowball flies, it hits the cat,
Oh, what a disaster! Imagine that!
Winds whisper secrets of chilly cheer,
As hot cocoa dribbles, oh dear, oh dear!

Frosty puppets smile from afar,
Excited kids scream like rock stars!
The snowmen squabble, who takes the lead?
One has a carrot, the other a seed!

So raise a toast to winter's glee,
With snowflakes swirling around the tree.
Chase the night with joyous delight,
In this wonderland, oh what a sight!